# Bodylines

*poems by*

# Tereza Joy Kramer

*Finishing Line Press*
Georgetown, Kentucky

# Bodylines

ACKNOWLEDGMENTS

With appreciation to the editors of the following journals and anthologies for
publishing these poems:

*Cicada*: untitled "My sweet, thin …"
*Elements*, Slipstream Press: "Bodylines."
*Journal for Compressed Creative Arts:* "nude."
*Her Mark 2004*, Woman Made Gallery, Chicago: "Love."
*Migrants and Stowaways*, Knoxville Writers Guild: "Greens and Browns."
*Open 24 Hours*: "Shelters" and "Shotgun Shells."
*Remembering the Days That Breathed Pink*, Quaci Press: "Hospital Netting,"
"Loneliness," "Perimeter," and "Tulips Unfolding."
*103: The Image Warehouse:* "You Push the Merry-go-round."
*Not a Muse: the inner lives of women*, Haven Books: "Aproned Dots" and "The
First Was a Girl."

Thank you also to Gallery One in Ellensburg, Washington, for the exhibit of art
and poems in which "Aproned Dots" first appeared.


Publisher: Leah Maines
Editor: Christen Kincaid
Cover Art: Ana Arroyo Kramer
Author Photo: Raquel Arroyo Kramer
Cover Design: Tereza Joy Kramer


Printed in the USA on acid-free paper.
Order online:  www.finishinglinepress.com
            also available on amazon.com

Author inquiries and mail orders:
Finishing Line Press
P. O. Box 1626
Georgetown, Kentucky 40324
U. S. A.

# Table of Contents

*for Ana, Raquel, and all my other teachers*

My sweet, thin breast milk
    squirts across our wooden floor.
        The dog licks, wants more.

**Shelters**

A woman writes about families who pass
through homeless shelters down south
somewhere, but not in one of the many
places she's failed

to stay, trapped
by those who ask too much.
For she is always leaving
sadness, and the suffering
that teaches her
structures
are unimportant.

She sits in one of four rooms of one of
the smallest places she's ever lived,
crowded by the work and play of two
daughters who want their big house back,

don't want the her that she's becoming.
And she has no man she really knows
and no friends in the shelter of
these new woods she thinks she loves.

**Love**

My daughter screams that I'm
The Worst Mom In The World.

She's right! Who else would slap
away a child's kick? Who else,
when told at high pitch in the face
to Shut Up would let palm disappear
into fist, no thought, and tremble?

Phone in hand, she starts to dial 911
as taught in school, this being whose
rage birthed her and now
takes me to a new fine line.

**Dying Yesterday**


How could Egyptian stone exist—
  3,000 years later in this
   museum in Saint Louis Missouri,

Flowers spiraling forever
  on a shoulder's back,
Sculpted language buried
  and resurrected—

If we, too, could learn to walk
  as though
  we'd died yesterday,

Then every day would be—

Accumulating moments—
  of gift,
  the eternal breath and step—
  over
    and
      over
       and

## Staged

Eight thick back and across the stage,
on curved rows of arranged chairs,
all in regal black: these college students
of music written centuries before.

Arms move furtively, eyes
on sheets of music and their favorite
conductor embodying
the movement of creation.

Their thin, tuned, energetic faces
are intently ignorant
that 95 out of 99 won't ever play for money
and 98 won't get jobs like their mentor's.

Some 10 will become music teachers,
wishing they'd tried harder
or applied to more places, not moved steadily
away from freshness,
away from something always scary —
as if they could have made a difference.

There's one cellist on stage with thinning hair
and a frumpy midsection. There are
empty seats beside her. She's filling in
to help the kids sound better.
During bows, she's the only one looking out,
really looking at us.
The young around her are levitated
by applause, the feeling of praise
inside their own selves, ready to be ripe,
ready to make a difference,
no idea, really—

## Tulips Unfolding

A photographer friend sends me
the still lifes he's shot on contract
for billboards: Saint Catherine's
Hospital for Women & Children.

They'd mailed him tulips from Holland,
boxes and boxes, to ensure the idea
blooms and buds, all the right
stages. My old friend, frustrated
in marriage and art, hopes I will see
what marketing execs could not

maybe a flaw behind a
burnt-orange petal, or fear
in a muted green leaf with
veins too numerous to count or
to see, reaching, exploring.

Tomorrow, my teen-age daughter
will lie prone inside
a state-of-the-art MRI cylinder
while I, hands not writing
in the next room, watch
a computer render her brain,
light up the hidden
reaches in shadowy neon.

Doctors call this a precaution.
They need to understand
her sudden inability to hear
in one ear, to know whether
there's something pressing
that could cause, very soon,
the right side of her smooth face
to droop,

so that she will begin
to turn shyly and hope that all
anyone will ever see,
as she walks the other way,
is a waving cadence of hair
she spends an hour perfecting
each morning.

**Greens and Browns**

The greens and browns of this
pre-teen's flip-flops are lighter
than the tones of earth in spring.
She angles her rubber sandals
to tamp down the seeds.
Her toes slide as she works—
the little one slips entirely
off the edge, into wet dirt;
the next one hugs her sandal's
half-inch rubber.

She straightens, taps the hoe
into her palm, and says:
We're going to have lots of surprises
this summer.

Mud is creeping up over The Gap
and between all of her toes—longer
this year, almost adult-size.
By mid-morning, the caked brown
is half-dried and half-dark.

## The First Was a Girl

I saw a lizard
as big as from my hand
to my elbow.
It had hair like mine,
red eyes, clothes.
        It could talk.

Two others
had blonde hair, red eyes, glasses,
a suit:
twin boys.
The first was a girl,
my twin.

I tried to lock the doors
but couldn't.
They came inside.
Maybe it's like the way
        I can see ghosts.

Maybe they were the ghosts
of the lizard,
the dead lizard
I found
in the back yard.
I picked it up by its tail,
scared Irene with it.
Some boys smashed it.

They said
        I killed it,
and that I killed the hummingbird
and the other baby bird.
        I didn't.
I tried to teach the babies to fly.

§

**Turn**

tulips fold inward against
the evening's cold, conserve—
I long for this instinct—
smart, tender—
so unlike my stubborn
push—
I need to learn
how to shutter in before frost

## Bodylines

Driving from our new home
into town, you and me, we take
the curves on Giant City Road—

where cyclists out for healthy Sundays
put lives at risk along white lines.
Conversation lulls. You ask

if I'd read the story in the paper
of a minister, sentenced
to 30 years. She was fourteen

when it started. Ridiculous case,
you say. I feel burning rise
in my chest and a shiver deep

within my arms. You don't get it—
you, who hold me if I convulse
under incest recalled, molten iron

beneath the trapdoor, my own story
invisible over all my body.
You continue: How can she

accuse him … now? It went on for
years, after she was underage …
I try to explain, logically like a man,

that things get all mixed up, that it
takes years to know, real.
Is it important that you agree?

My forearms ache. I have
carpal tunnel—a syndrome
of repetitive motion. Cool consultants

blame the keyboards I type on, editing
horrors of the world for readers
of black-and-white headlines.

But as things get less sure I suspect
my loss of strength began
gripping the metal sides

of a collapsible bed
in Dad's vacation home
because the same tendons ache

whenever I approach that place
where men cannot fathom, where even
with the man I want this morning

I doubt if love and grace
can coexist—maybe only
in the perfect logic

of sidewalks, predictability,
sun and rain, where nothing
can happen in between.

## For Gertrude

Her friends knew most the bare facts,
had read the paper and heard Granny tell
just a bit
      of what the coroner found,

but today they're in court, learning
a shoe print on swollen eyes
was so deep the tread
led cops to the killers. No one knows
if she died of frostbite
or the vomit stuck
in her windpipe.
When the rapes occurred,
the men testify,
      she was alive enough to cry.

Her brother, 12, can't talk.
Her best friend, 17, knows she's the one
who let her leave with those guys.
She twirls growing-out bangs
and listens to lawyers in three-piece suits,
lawyers who tell her to hold on,
      hold back her testimony.

## The Grain Bin

Mice appear through dust of cow feed
she scoops into buckets.

Their nails rasp the wooden floor,
bare between bits of feed.

Two farmhands come
to the door, block her light.

Take your clothes off.
Now.

No,
she laughs.

You think this is a game?
They step inside

the frame.
Come here.

**Shotgun Shells**

*A response to "The Smell of the Sea," by Larry Levis*

Two men rape her, one by one,
make the boyfriend watch, kill them both.
The poet tells of a second man's torture,
details each moment toward that death.

This is written by a man, about men, not
of the pain of her, eyes wide open.

I stare into the reflection of my chair,
reclining beside a lake in a woods.

How would Earth recover from this.

What can never be redeemed—
spent shotgun shells on brown
leaves. Season upon season

man-molded brass remains
stuck to red plastic
exploded open at the point.

§

## Hospital Netting

Millions of insect wings
create falling folds of translucent
net I'm warned to leave be.

The nurses away,
my fingers search,
shaking, finding
an opening to touch
your unsteady breath, your
barely sleeping cheeks
two weeks from my womb.

We share a space
beyond fear
of illness or oxygen tent,
of all the rock-solid
veils that will ever block
my caring for you

      \*\*\*

like today
as I sit on the edge of a motel bed
watching the sky go gray,
then black, hanging on
to the last unreal glimpse
of beige stuccoed concrete,
the juvenile rehab
center,

recalling
how the neonatal ICU
nurse told me that if
you survived, you'd always
be gasping for breath.

## How Many Fingertips

I rhythmically rub
index finger against thumb tip,
thinking it's the source of pain—last
month's cut throbbing again—
while the firm edge of palm
steers the wheel. I drive, drive
three new hours toward
my daughter's third
rehab center,
pull over to check
the route and notice
a thin cut in a second finger,
this one fresh, red. Which
incident opened it up?

My sliver of reading glasses
reveal that all my fingers
are rough, their tips
dry and jagged
as though rubbed too hard,
too many times.

No one
gets to be raw alone.

## Two Letters from the County Jail

Back home from leaving her
in rehab again,
I start cleaning her room,
the dark stale smell
of pot and who knows
what else, find two letters,
handwritten.

*Hope you're doing pretty damn good.*
*Send me good vibes on the 27th—*
*my birthday.*

*Always do what is best for you*
*and you will never be sorry—*

How dare he mail advice
to my teen-age girl.

*My mind is in a good spot*
*and I am ready*
*for my world to change,*
*stop hurting myself.*

She'd stayed in contact
every time
he'd broken parole.
She told me
they were always only friends.

*I pray you get a chance to grab those books,*
*I would cry if I lost them—*

She and I had gone in,
his apartment door unlocked,
and recovered stacks of books,
good ones I'd been meaning
to read—on philosophy, ways to live
a meaningful life.

*Feel horrible for the pain*
*I caused everyone.*

The second letter is dated
the day before
he'd killed himself.

*Please pass along my address*
*to anyone*
*who might know*
*how to use the postal system.*

*Most the inmates are morons.*
*I had to show several of them*
*how to address an envelope.*
*No kidding.*

*Thank you for taking Fluffy.*

Yes, we'd saved his cat.
He'd thought ahead,
left water in the bathtub,
an overflowing scattering
of food.

§

**morning on the forest floor**


too much too many
ferns to write about to
hide their
blue effervescence and
millions of tiny suns in
depths and crevices of
all the layers of greens

how can sun be on the ground

where
do we hide

is there no
dark safe world of womb

far from those
who would share our selves

take and make
us rise
just like
the damned persistent ferns
        freshly green and
up again this year

from the deep center
of dull brown twirls
that would crackle into dust
        into nothing
        at a touch

## The Hair Poem

Strands so fine, so easily tangled.
Nature needs levity to curl.

Swirls of brown to blonde stick
to my porcelain tub

and the thick teeth
of a pink, oversized comb.

I collect them, create a little being,
shiny with water and conditioner, the size

of a baby mouse. These I had carried
on me, so many months

of half-an-inch-a-month progression
into mature something—

where do they go now?
A boyfriend suggested

I throw them into the yard
for birds. Good nesting material.

Another shoved a clump
into his pocket. For him,

I had cut a perfectly spiraled

blonde tip, but he'd left it on
my dresser—better last night's

tangles caught forever in the comb.
This is single at 40:

bathroom clumps getting bigger,
the size of full-grown mice.

I hope it's only the impact
of supplements to maintain

muscles, keep running like I'm only
30, also good for joints.

The doctor bets arthritis
down deep inside my butt bone,

where the hinge of a hip
sometimes locks me still,

like when exercising
or other stressed positions.

## Loneliness

Miniature brown ants appear
inside the lined cabinets
in my efficiency kitchen and also
behind the bathroom mirror—
the narrow glass shelves
and the tube of white cream
I use to make
hairs disappear from upper lip
before anyone can see them
increasing in number
every year I'm here.

One rogue ant
is exploring
the textured terrain
of my imperfect pillow
as I pull from its linen case—
to breathe freely after a night
of menopausal sweat.

May they find no fault
to build a colony
upon or within.

May I observe them freely
without crushing
a single one—
no fat thumb or forefinger.

May I place not even one
of the little round orange
innocuous looking
plastic traps. May I wish
the ants may scout
their own oblivious way
toward death.

**With Fear**

The biggest part of my head, the back,
sticks to pillow. Heavy.
I recall a mantra of birds rising.
Happiness, light.

What's wrong
with moments of despair?

They expand
into brick-thick black walls
that can stretch
into gray, widening, thinning,
on and on into and through

invisibility. All clear,
every morning—

## Perimeter

Mother is sustained by her sunroom:
glassed-in cage of miniatures
of the farm she once ran—the

fields of grain, garden, wooded hills,
the cows she'd buy, then calculate
how soon to send to slaughter.

We walk her perimeter of glass,
stop to rest and water
the soils. She tells her stories

of acquiring each plastic, ceramic,
or hand-cradled clay, how each plant
has grown, how it experiences this day.

As she talks, she looks straight
into me. Her eyes are full. Her
pupils are brilliant, deep,
and ringed by vacant blue.

## Aproned Dots

Dots, dots, dots, dots
crushed and pulled and starched
into vertical seams and
bands of horizontal error,
all regular as it should be.

The cloth of this apron
is translucent too.
I hang it in my window frame,
writing, breaking
lines into immortality
across a little page.

Outside, parallel to lines of hanging
fabric, are falling
soft white dots of snow, each
its own design, each
its own control.

Avalanches
of white chaos incarnate
are busy out there closing roads,
boxing us into one small town.

I want to take a long walk, tongue out,
let silently indefinable dots
envelope me as they vanish,
hiding my profile gently so I
can laugh at the cars
sliding into my earthly body.

**nude**

a creek's broken ice reflects
the chipped whiteness
of a lone sycamore trunk
utterly unself-conscious
reaching up
holding on inside

Tereza Joy Kramer grew up in Ohio and began her journalism career at Ohio University, working as a news reporter for *The Post*. After college, she reported for United Press International in Mexico City. Journalism later took her to the Texas border, where her two daughters were born, and then to Indiana, where she began writing poems and discovered the world of art. She owes a debt of gratitude to leaders of the RopeWalk Writers Retreat, Indiana University Writers Conference, First Mondays critique group, the Evansville Writers Bloc, the Dadapalooza / Mamapalooza performative readings, and the Owensboro Third Tuesday Coffeehouse. Inspired by so many artists, Tereza Joy pursued a Master of Fine Arts in poetry at Southern Illinois University Carbondale. She particularly enjoyed creating and performing a live exhibit, "i," at The Glove Factory with other MFA artists and poets, and reading for "Women's Issues," a *Linen Weave of Themes* series on WFHB Radio in Bloomington.

Tereza Joy also discovered she enjoyed teaching and so pursued a PhD in rhetoric and composition, also at SIUC. She and her family then moved to Ellensburg, Washington, where she taught and directed the University Writing Center. From there, they relocated to the Bay Area, where she currently teaches and directs the Center for Writing Across the Curriculum at Saint Mary's College of California.

Tereza Joy's poems have appeared in a number of journals, including *Cicada, The Iguana Review, 103 The Image Warehouse, The Journal of Compressed Creative Arts, Open 24 Hours,* and *Re)verb*. Her work also has been published in the anthologies *Elements*, Slipstream Press; *Her Mark*, Chicago Women Made Gallery; *Migrants and Stowaways*, Knoxville Writers Guild; *Not a Muse: the inner lives of women*, Haven Books; *Poetic Voices Without Borders*, Gival Press; *Remembering the Days That Breathed Pink*, Quaci Press; and *Regrets Only: Contemporary Poets on the Theme of Regret*, Little Pear Press.

www.ingramcontent.com/pod-product-compliance
Lightning Source LLC
LaVergne TN
LVHW041328080426
835513LV00008B/631